WORKING IN THE UN FAMILY: NEW JOB NEW YOU

How to write a job application that will get you noticed

Gwyneth Letherbarrow

The information you'll find in this book is to educate you. We make no promise or guarantee of income or earnings.

All rights reserved. No parts of this book may be used or reproduced in any manner without written permission except in the case of brief quotations in articles or reviews.

Please visit www.feelgoodcoachingandconsulting.com to find out more.

Copyright Gwyneth Letherbarrow 2018

ISBN-13: 978-1985756953
ISBN-10: 1985756951

Contents

FOREWORD 1

INTRODUCTION 4

    How to use this book 5

    What else? 5

ONE - KNOWING WHAT YOU WANT 6

    Room for compromise? 9

TWO - WHERE SHOULD YOU LOOK FOR YOUR JOB? 15

THREE - WHY SHOULD THE HIRING MANAGER CHOOSE TO INTERVIEW YOU? 20

FOUR - GATHERING THE FACTS 25

FIVE - PAINT YOUR PICTURE 39

    The Letter of Motivation 43

SIX - BRINGING IT ALL TOGETHER 47

SEVEN - RESULT! 48

    A final note on social media 48

QUESTIONS AND ANSWERS 50

ADDITIONAL READING AND USEFUL LINKS 52

ABOUT THE AUTHOR 54

FOREWORD

At the end of 2012 I was holding a CV writing and interview skills workshop for an organisation that was faced with yet another restructuring and downsizing exercise. One of the participants told me that he was very worried about his future because he was one of several people doing the same job, and he was going to have to re-apply for his own position.

He was convinced that another colleague was going to get the job because they got on with the boss better than he did. He seemed close to despair. He worked hard at the workshop but I could see that he still had a lot of questions that only he could find the answers to, about himself, and about his employer.

Some six months later during a workshop at the same organisation, I received a message that a young man had asked to talk to me during the coffee break.

I didn't recognize the confident, smiling face as he entered the room. "I got the job", he said, "thank you for changing my life". I was amazed, and overjoyed. This was the same young man who had previously seemed so close to giving up on himself. He told me that although a lot of what I taught went against what he had previously believed, he was willing to change and had worked hard at rebranding himself, with great success.

Back to the present day. Levels of unemployment are not likely to decrease drastically anywhere in the world any time soon. Society is on a mad upwards spiral demanding that we have more and more academic qualifications, and yet we hear about an increasing number of graduates unable to find work.

Everywhere I go people tell me that you 'have to know someone' if you want to get a job, or they say 'unemployment is so high, I don't stand a chance'. More recently there appears to be a growing trend towards 'young professionals' taking unpaid internships for several years to gain work experience.

But even they are complaining that competition is too tough and that it's difficult to get a place. At the same time if you look in a newspaper or on the internet you will see hundreds of vacancies, yet organisations grumble about the fact that they cannot find 'qualified' staff.

So what is happening? Technology is happening, worker's rights are happening, globalisation is happening, age discrimination is happening (even though the law says it is not allowed to happen), need I go on?

What remains the same however is the fact that it is up to YOU to take action. There is no quick solution or magic formula, and there are no guarantees. However, this book contains the same content I use in my workshops and so I know that these steps can produce impressive results for anyone who is prepared to do the work, and regardless of the position you want.

It wasn't me who changed the life of the young man I briefly described, he did it all himself because he focused on where he wanted to be, and then worked out how to get there by getting clear on how to market himself.

And if he can do it, then so can you. Good luck!

New Job New You

INTRODUCTION

A job application is a CV in a specific format, and the dictionary will give you a definition that runs along the lines of it being a historical record of your skills, qualifications and employment; the words 'Curriculum Vitae' translate as 'the course of one's life'.

All well and good, but your job application is so much more than a summary of your experience. It is a business proposal and your very own form of marketing because it describes YOU! Your potential employer probably has no idea who you are, and your application needs to stand out if you want to get an interview.

There is a fantastic graphic on www.businessinsider.com that shows the parts of a CV that the person looking at it will focus on the first time they see it. In general – and please remember that this may well be someone in the Human Resources office who is looking at hundreds of applications – their eyes will look at your personal details, your profile, your most recent job if you had one, your highest level of academic achievement, and there they will stop!

On average, the first person to look at your CV or application will spend just *six seconds* making up their minds as to whether you deserve closer scrutiny.

So if you knew you have the time it takes to read this sentence to convince someone that you are worth a second look, and considering that your application had the power to change your entire future career path, how much time would you spend preparing it? A couple of hours, or maybe a couple of days?

Have you ever been tempted to find a CV writing service to do the work for you because it's just too difficult or it takes too long to do it yourself? How much do you want the job?

The CV that I currently use when marketing my workshops has taken me the best part of three years to refine, and every time I send it out it gets changed again to 'fit' with the person or company that it is going to.

You are unique, as is your future employer, which is why you must adapt your application to the needs of each position and before you do that, you must know what you want, why you want it, and why someone would hire you.

How to use this book

You will find that each of the activities in this book form building blocks that are going to help you create a job application for an organisation in the UN family that gets you noticed for the right reasons.

Get yourself a notebook and pen or pencil to make notes because nothing is set in stone, and you may find yourself wanting to go back and make changes to your work.

Whilst the step-by-step process is easy to follow, be honest with yourself about what you want and what you're good at. Take time to reflect, and if you're unsure about what to do next, instead of applying logic to your decisions, pay attention to how you *feel* about your ideas. You may be surprised by some of the insights you have.

What else?

Having worked in international organisations for more than 20 years, I have heard all the complaints about political appointments, unfair recruitment procedures, discrimination and lots more. On several occasions I also found myself being told by others about what I could or could not do, and with one exception I successfully challenged those wanting to limit my progress.

It's up to you to do the work in this book and to invest in yourself. Don't fall victim to what others tell you about what is possible and what is not, because it's rare that anyone will be able to show you a written policy or administrative instruction to back up their restricting comments. Be accountable and take responsibility for the fabulous future that you deserve.

I'd love it if you decided that you wanted to connect on LinkedIn, and you'll also find a lot of resources on my website at www.feelgoodcoachingandconsulting.com

Onwards!

ONE - KNOWING WHAT YOU WANT

"Begin with the end in mind" – Stephen Covey

If you knew that success was guaranteed, what would you do? If you didn't have to worry about what your family thought or deal with the consequences of your choice, which career path would you choose?

Some people applying to organisations in the UN family believe that they are under pressure to find a job purely for the sake of being able to pay the bills.

And a significant number of people don't bother to apply for a job that they really want because they have convinced themselves that they aren't clever enough or that competition is too tough, or that someone else has already been selected because they are 'sitting' on the position.

And then there are those who apply for anything and everything because they believe that by doing so they are increasing their chances of success.

Fair enough.

But that is no excuse to submit the same application for five or even 50 positions, and then wonder why you aren't being invited for an interview. The application process must begin with you, and not the job vacancy notice.

Do you know what is important to you? Do you know what you love to do and the type of people you enjoy working with?

If you love being around other people, working in a friendly yet fast moving environment and have the patience to do repetitive work, you might be happiest organising internal meetings or high-level conferences; You are never going to be happy working as a political officer who spends the majority of their time reading and writing reports.

By the same token, if you are someone who is a stickler for detail, good at analysis and drafting policy documents, and you enjoy some solitude, you will more likely be suited to work in the legal or financial professions. You would probably be miserable having to manage others who constantly made demands on your time.

Clearly these are sweeping statements, and they serve only to demonstrate the importance of you understanding which environment you will best thrive in, so that you enjoy your work, and give your best.

So before we move on, if you are the type of person who loves to travel, or perhaps you're very creative and love variety, think very carefully about whether you really want to work for the UN …

It is made up of well-established organisations with solid structures and hierarchies, and although I have worked with many clients who were happy to 'fit in' with the chain of command and bureaucracy, some of them discovered that there were other ways in which they could fulfil their sense of purpose without having to compromise their love of independence.

As you work through the exercises pay close attention to how you feel about your answers. Be authentic and be true to yourself.

EXERCISE 1

Start off by writing a list of everything you love to do. Think back to when you were a child. Did you love to dance, or read books, or play in the garden? What was it about those activities that made them fun? What do you enjoy doing now? What do other people tell you you're good at, even if it seems so easy to you that it doesn't seem important?

I LOVE:

_____

_____

_____

_____

_____

_____

EXERCISE 2

Now write down EVERYTHING that your dream job would include. Get into as much detail as you possibly can to the extent that you can imagine yourself already doing work that you love. Here are some questions to answer to start you off:

- Which organisation would you love to work with and why?
- What does the organisation do that interests you?
- What sort of people work there?
- What do you want to do there – are you working in a support or management role?
- Which of your skills are you using?
- Which policies does the organisation have in place to support its staff?
- What are your working hours?
- How much do you want to earn (don't sell yourself short but be realistic)?
- Which benefits would you like to receive?
- What does your office or working space look like?
- What will you place on your desk?

The list can be as long or as short as you would like it to be, but take time to identify every aspect of what is important to you about a job, and write it down.

BRAINSTORM and DARE TO DREAM because it's free !

_____

_____

_____

_____

_____

_____

_____

Room for compromise?

We generally tend to scour job vacancy notices very briefly, looking at those that sort of fit what we can do. By deciding beforehand what is important to *you*, you will have a better idea of what you want.

If you find yourself in a job that you don't love, where you don't feel appreciated and you're not using your skills, the chances are that you will eventually become miserable, and I have never met anyone who wants to be miserable all the time.

You might not believe that you can have everything that you want. So could you compromise on your journey time or working hours? Or is spending time with your family in the evenings an important part of your day that you are not willing to give up?

You may find that by the end of this next activity that you have changed your mind about some items on your list and that's fine. Be aware of how you feel about each of your choices and follow your instincts.

EXERCISE 3

Your two lists from Exercises 1 and 2 will already have given you a better idea of the direction you want to go in. You now need to put your list in order of priority so that when you start your job search you know where areas of potential compromise might be (or not).

Start off by comparing the first two items on your list (which will be much longer than the one here). Which of those two are more important to you? Put a cross or a tick next to the item that you choose.

In the example here I have decided that it would be more important to earn EUR 3000 per month than to work for the IAEA. Having to decide between boxes one and three, my choice would be box three, to work 30 hours per month. Then I compare box one with box four, box one with box five, box one with box six, and so on.

I want to work for the IAEA	
I want to earn EUR 3000 per month	X
I want to work 30 hours per month	X
I love talking to people	
I want to begin work at 9:30	
I want private health insurance	
I love spending time outside	

Then you repeat the process by comparing box two with box three, box two with box four, box two with box five … then move to box three and compare it with box four, box three with box five … then move to box four and compare it with box five … keep going until you have worked your way through the entire list, always marking the statement that is more important.

My example ends up looking like this:

1.	I want to work for the IAEA	
2.	I want to earn EUR 3000 per month	X X X X
3.	I want to work 30 hours per month	X X X X
4.	I love talking to people	X X X X X X
5.	I want to begin work at 9:30	X
6.	I want private health insurance	X X X X
7.	I love spending time outside	X X

What I have learned from this is that although I thought that working for the IAEA was quite important to me, in comparison to the other things I want, it has become completely irrelevant. I have also learned that I would probably be happy to have a longer journey to work if the other things I wanted were in place.

I now feel more comfortable about considering other organisations which offer me the things I want, and won't waste any more time and energy only looking in one direction.

Now it's your turn. Put all your statements into the following table – add more pieces of paper if necessary. By the time you have finished you will be able to see the most important elements of the job that *you love* and you will know what to look for when looking at vacancy notices.

1.		
2.		
3.		
4.		
5.		
6.		
7.		
8.		
9.		
10.		
11.		
12.		
13.		

14.		
15.		
16.		
17.		
18.		
19.		
20.		

EXERCISE 4

Have you ever labelled yourself with a job title, for example secretary, or solicitor, or marketer, or manager? That isn't who you are. If you met Richard Branson or Oprah Winfrey, or the Secretary-General of the United Nations in the elevator and had 30 seconds to describe yourself, what would you say? Think in terms of the results that you deliver.

_____

_____

_____

_____

_____

"Your work is going to fill a large part of your life, and the only way to be truly satisfied is to do what you believe is great work. The only way to do great work is to LOVE what you do." Steve Jobs

NOTES AND GREAT IDEAS

Gwyneth Letherbarrow

TWO - WHERE SHOULD YOU LOOK FOR YOUR JOB?

"If opportunity doesn't knock, build a door." – Milton Berle

Are you the kind of person who sits at home and spends hours searching for jobs on the internet, not talking to anyone? You might just be lucky one day and find something amazing, but it can be quite demotivating to cut yourself off from the world just because you are unemployed.

If you hear of somebody having been 'headhunted' or offered a job, it's probably because someone told someone else who told someone else that they did their job really well. When did you last do some networking?

I'm not talking about going to formal networking events – although of course that might be an option – I'm talking about spending time with your friends and contacts and asking them if they could let you know if they hear of any job openings.

Give them a good idea about what it is you are looking for because if you have taken your time with Step One, you will know what you want.

In addition to the platforms of the individual organisations, there are a lot of websites that list job opportunities within the UN family - but you could spend a lot of time looking at a screen and reading a lot of generic and boring job vacancy notices.

- Try entering the title of the job you want and the organisation and town (or country) where you want to work in your internet search engine and see what comes up;
- Upload your profile (with a professional photograph) onto LinkedIn including key words that are relevant to the type of job you're looking for;
- Network online by joining LinkedIn groups. You will frequently see that users share vacancy notices for jobs available in their section or department.

Don't expect a job to land in your lap just because you have great qualifications and experience. Any job search is going to require you to communicate with others on a regular basis.

EXERCISE 5

Write down all your ideas about how you can market yourself and to whom.

_____

_____

_____

_____

_____

_____

Who do you know who already has the type of job that you would love to do? Who could you tell that you are looking for a job? What are you going to tell them?

_____

_____

_____

_____

Move out of your comfort zone! What's the worst thing that could happen to you if you dared to dream, to do something new or different? Put another way, what will you be feeling or thinking next year or in five years' time if you don't take action now?

_____

_____

_____

_____

EXERCISE 6

Create your very own marketing plan. Imagine you were going to be launching a brilliant new product that people had been waiting to buy for months. What are the steps that you need to take?

Activity	Start Date	Planned End Date	Done
For example: Set up LinkedIn Profile	20/11	22/11	
Join three LinkedIn groups	1/12	1/12	

Activity	Start Date	Planned End Date	Done

NOTES AND GREAT IDEAS

New Job New You

THREE - WHY SHOULD THE HIRING MANAGER CHOOSE TO INTERVIEW YOU?

"What lies before us and what lies behind us are very little compared to
what lies within us" – Ralph Waldo Emerson

Assuming that the computer programme has selected your application to be more closely scrutinised (more about this later), you now know that you have around six or seven seconds to convince the relevant human to invite you for interview. You are going to have to present something special to stand out from the others in the pile and get their attention.

When it comes to marketing or branding yourself, I like to use the example of washing products. Think back to the last time you saw an advertisement for some washing powder or fabric conditioner. Did an actor stand there with the product in their hands and say 'this washes well, please buy it'? Probably not.

Instead you will have seen smiling faces, people dancing, the sun shining, children running around, bright colours, clean washing … Do you see where I'm going with this? It's not enough to tell your potential employer about what you can do, you have to be able to paint a picture for them about how you approach your work so that they can already imagine you standing (or sitting) in front of them.

We tend to plan much of our lives in terms of the next few days or weeks, and sometimes we'll book a holiday a few months in advance, but all too often we do not give the same level of attention to planning our middle-term and long-term future careers.

Where do you want to be in five years' time (which by the way is one of the questions you could be asked at interview)? What do you do really well? What are your achievements? How are you going to sell yourself? What is your 'brand'?

When answering these questions you may be tempted to put yourself into a 'box' and call yourself an accountant, a project manager, or a nuclear safety expert. But that isn't who you are. They are merely titles and don't mean very much on paper. You want the person reading your application to be able to *feel* how it might be to work with you.

Here's another question. How does your definition of 'qualified' differ from that of your potential employer's? How many times have you said yourself or heard others say that a person should not have been selected for a position because they were not qualified?

You may be at the point where you have decided that your work experience and academic qualifications just about meet the requirements of the job vacancy. But equally important is *your personality,* because by the time you get to interview, the hiring team has already decided that on paper at least, you match the job profile. The question to be answered is, do they like you ?!

Can you can be trusted? Are you detail oriented? Do you work well in a team, or do you prefer working on your own initiative? Do you like a routine or do you get bored easily? How do you handle disagreements at work? How good are you at persuading others? How would you deal with a mistake that you made? How do you deal with deadlines and stress? How important is it to you to follow the 'policies and rules' of the organisation?

Which *specific examples* can you give for all these qualities and skills?

None of these are likely to be easy questions to address, and they will take some time to answer. You are unique, and if you want to market yourself successfully then you absolutely must know *what you do well* before you start writing your application.

Remember that you have just seconds to convince someone to put your application onto the 'for interview' pile. By painting a picture of 'you', the human being, you are going to stand out from the other 95 per cent of applicants who have simply copied and pasted a list of their previous tasks and responsibilities. Get it all out of your brain and onto paper.

EXERCISE 7

My brand is:

_____

_____

_____

_____

_____

NOTES AND GREAT IDEAS

FOUR - GATHERING THE FACTS

"Get your facts first, then you can distort them as you please." – Mark Twain

One reason for candidates submitting poor applications is because they have launched into completing the online application form before they were clear on what they were going to write.

Before you even type your name in the relevant online portal, it's a good idea to pull together *everything* you need. Advance preparation will also mean that if the online system goes down or doesn't save your data, you have a back-up. By all means print off an empty form so that you know which types of data are required, but avoid disaster by working offline first.

You are going to produce a fairly long document and you will find it much easier to chop and change things around according to the needs of each application if you do the hard work now.

EXERCISE 8

Create a 'word' or similar document (or use this book) and add your answers for all the following.

YOUR PERSONAL DETAILS

Telephone number
Where can you be contacted easily? If there are small children or elderly relatives at home, you might *not* want to include that number. It is very frustrating for a person working in human resources who calls to arrange an interview only to be met with the first words of a three-year old.

By the same token, giving your current work telephone number could mean that a colleague picks up the telephone when you aren't there, and that could prove embarrassing if your job search is a secret.

Email address
Consider setting up an email address specifically for your job search. This will help you to keep track of where you have applied and when, instead of having to search through other personal correspondence. What image do you want to project?

Use something relevant such as your full name, or the first initial of your first name followed by your family name, or a similar format. Take care too with numbers as it is difficult to tell the difference between the letter 'l', and the number '1' – make sure that the email address is easy to read.

Most companies and organisations have an email/internet policy that will include a rule about using it for official purposes only, and using your work email address (if you are currently employed) for job applications could backfire.

If there were justification to do so, your employer could have access to your email account, and if you have not told anyone about your job search, you could find yourself leaving your job earlier than anticipated. This would of course be an extreme case, but keep it in mind.

Skype
It costs nothing to set up a Skype account on the internet, and this can be very useful information to include if you are looking at working overseas, or even just want to cut down on your telephone bills.

Date of birth
According to EU legislation an employer is not allowed to ask for your date of birth during the application process, unless it can be proved that it is relevant to the work in question. You will be aware however that the employer will be able to guess your approximate age from the information you provide about your education, and UN organisations still include this box on their application forms.

Marital status and dependents
Again, this is not relevant to your ability to do a job, but the UN requires that you include this information.

Telephone   _____

Email address: _____

Skype: _____

YOUR PROFILE (look back to Exercises 4 and 7)
How are you going to describe yourself? This will be relevant to your cover letter or letter of motivation

_____

_____

_____

_____

_____

Career history
State the names and addresses of previous employers (if applicable), and your dates of employment in reverse chronological order (ie.,include the most recent first). Describe your key duties and responsibilities (we are going to look at how you present that information a little later).

Which examples can you use to describe your activities? Find examples of what you did well, how your input made a difference (ask yourself the question 'so what?'), and write down everything you can think of that is going to help paint your picture.

Education
List the details of university or college courses including the grade achieved, and your dates of study. Include the most recent first.

Professional membership
If you are in the medical profession you may belong to the Medical Council, or if you work in finance you may belong to one of the Chartered Institutes.

Training and development
Make a list of all the courses you have studied which were not a part of your formal education for example career coaching, or IT packages, or even training with the Red Cross as a volunteer.

Publications
This will usually be more relevant to positions requiring very specific qualifications in the medical, legal or educational sectors.

Voluntary work
Have you taken part in any activities to support others?

Other information
Most employers will want to know whether you have a valid driving licence and/or speak other languages, as well as which software packages you are familiar with.

Career history

Most recent job/dates

_____

Contact details of supervisor (if applicable)

_____

_____

What did you do?

_____

_____

_____

What did you do well (relevant examples)?

_____

_____

Next job and dates

_____

Contact details of supervisor (if applicable)

_____

_____

What did you do?

_____

_____

_____

What did you do well (relevant examples)?

_____

_____

Next job and dates

_____

Contact details of supervisor (if applicable)

_____

_____

What did you do?

_____

_____

What did you do well (relevant examples?

Next job and dates

Contact details of supervisor (if applicable)

What did you do?

What did you do well (relevant examples)?

Next job and dates

_____

Contact details of supervisor (if applicable)

_____

_____

What did you do?

_____

_____

_____

_____

What did you do well (relevant examples)?

_____

_____

Next job and dates

_____

Contact details of supervisor (if applicable)

_____

_____

What did you do?

_____

_____

What did you do well (relevant examples)?

Education

University (if applicable)

Dates and Grade(s)

Subject(s) studied

College (if applicable)

Dates and Grade(s)

Subject(s) studied

High School (if applicable)

_____

Dates and Grade(s)

_____

Subject(s) studied

_____

Secondary/comprehensive school (if applicable)

_____

Dates and Grade(s)

_____

Subject(s) studied

_____

Professional membership

If you are in the medical profession you may belong to the Medical Council, or if you work in finance you may belong to one of the Chartered Institutes.

_____

_____

_____

Training and development

If you have attended a lot of training courses ensure that you only include details about those that are relevant to each job application.

_____

_____

_____

_____

_____

_____

_____

_____

Publications

_____

_____

_____

Voluntary work

Have you taken part in any activities to support and help others?

_____

_____

_____

Other information

Driving license and type

___

Languages (and levels)

___

Software packages

___

Anything else?

___

___

Referees

You must ask permission from the person you wish to use as a referee. Who could you ask? Are they familiar with your work experience, academic qualifications or character? Most employers will ask for three referees, but you might want to ask four or five people when you start your job search so that you can select those that can provide information that is *relevant* for the job in question. Put their names and contact details here:

Referee 1

_____

_____

Referee 2

_____

_____

Referee 3

_____

_____

Referee 4

_____

_____

Referee 5

_____

_____

NOTES AND GREAT IDEAS

FIVE - PAINT YOUR PICTURE

"Data! Data! Data!" he cried impatiently.
"I can't make bricks without clay." – Sherlock Holmes

You have assembled all the basic facts, in addition to having some good examples that describe your approach to work, which in turn will give your future employer an insight into your personality. But before you begin completing the online application form, there are a few additional considerations.

The majority of job vacancies will look something like this (although of course an employer's list will likely be much longer):

Example:

Tasks and responsibilities:
Provides clerical and administrative support to the team
Deals with telephone and email enquiries
Manages the departmental budget
Coordinates departmental projects
Manages the diary of the Director

Competences
Communications
Analysis
Teamwork

Necessary qualifications
College Diploma
Proven ability to manage projects
Minimum of two years' work experience
Excellent written and spoken communication skills in English

The employer will have included all that detail for a reason, and first and foremost you have to be able to match your working experience to what is required in the job to which you are applying.

You also need to know that the person or persons looking at your application will have read the job description or vacancy notice several times. They know what they are looking for and you need to catch their attention. It is therefore imperative that you do three things:

1. *Use key words included in the job description*, so if you have read 'attention to detail', you need to use the words 'attention to detail' in your application. Most organisations in the UN family will have programmed their recruitment software to look for key words and phrases to help make them an initial selection. If the software does not find the key words, you will not make it onto the interview pile.

2. Tasks and responsibilities are usually *listed in order of their importance* and you need to *list your previous experience in the same order*, or as close as possible.

For example, using the short description above, if the majority of time in your current job is spent working with Excel but you are also responsible for providing administrative support to a team of people, you should emphasise the administrative support aspect as much as possible, because 'manages the departmental budget' is third, and 'admin support' is at the top of the list that your potential employer has provided.

3. Regardless of the job you are applying for, be it an IT technician, the manager of a conference services, or an under-secretary-general, *how would you describe the person* you were looking for if you were the employer? Which characteristics would be important?

One client I worked with was applying for a job as a mediator, and they had used the word 'enthusiastic' in their application. When we talked about it they realised that 'enthusiastic' was not a good adjective and that by putting a picture together of what a good mediator looked like they came up with words like 'discreet', 'diplomatic', and 'sincere'. Which characteristics will the perfect employee have for the job that you want?

There's a lot of work to be done here, but it will be worth it when you get the call to invite you for interview.

EXERCISE 9

Vacancy 1.
_____

Keywords

_____

_____

Vacancy 2.
_____

Keywords

_____

_____

Vacancy 3.
_____

Keywords

_____

_____

Vacancy 4.
_____

Keywords
_____

_____

Vacancy 5.
_____

Keywords
_____

_____

As explained above, you must include information about your employment history that *matches* (to the extent possible) and is *relevant* to the job vacancy. Check back regularly over what you have written and ask yourself what type of *feeling* you're getting from your description.

Take a look at these two examples:

Example 1:
- Good communicator and works well in teams
- As head of section I managed a team of eight staff and together we successfully developed and implemented a training strategy resulting in increased sales

Example 2:
- Provided management recommendations to the Director of Human Resources
- Provided management recommendations to the Director of Human Resources which were subsequently implemented resulting in a reduction in the annual operational budget

If you compare the two sentences in each example you'll see that the first one in each is quite dry, and says what's in the box of washing powder, so to speak. It's just the technical information.

The second sentences tell the person reading the application how *well* the applicant did their previous job, without specifying those characteristics or abilities in detail. By providing examples of your achievements it *is* possible to show your potential employer that you are good at what you do.

Do some research on the organisation that you are applying to. What does their website or public information/press releases say about them? What values do you think they have and what sort of people work there? If you are really excited about the possibility of being a part of their team, which abilities and values do *you* have that match those of the organisation?

Sometimes there is a requirement to list your strengths and skills in separate sections of an application form, but this list will remain meaningless without giving specific and relevant examples.

Go through every line of text in your 'work experience section' (if you have one) and make sure that you have painted the brightest picture possible of what it is you can do.

The Letter of Motivation

Bearing in mind that you have approximately six seconds to attract the attention of that person in HR, a summary of who you are and what you are good at can be a quick way of encouraging the reader to give you a closer look.

Most organisations include this section of the application at the end of the document, but that doesn't mean that it will be the last section to be read. I know that some hiring managers go directly to the letter of motivation to help them decide whether they want to read the other 10 or 20 pages.

The letter of motivation (sometimes called a cover letter, and sometimes presented with the sentence 'tell us why you want this job') provides you with another great opportunity to include those all-important key words, and to let others know why *you* should be selected for interview.

Do not attempt to repeat or list everything included on your application.

Stick as closely as possible to the given word/character limit (it is usually not possible to exceed the limit) and split up your 'letter' as follows.

Introduce yourself. For example:

"In my capacity as a manager, throughout my working experience in a multi-national environment, my excellent inter-personal skills have contributed to the successful implementation of three training projects which supported staff to meet their professional objectives. In addition to my university studies I have trained as a 'Project Management Professional' (PMP) and I enjoy working with teams who are goal oriented and committed to producing results."

With these few lines you have told your potential employer that you are a great manager and communicator, that you are a good team player and can be relied upon to follow through on tasks.

Then move on to the main body of the letter. Choose the three skills that you believe to be most relevant to the position, and describe them using specific examples so that you answer the question 'why do you want the job' and how they will help you make a valuable contribution. For example:

"One of the things that I have enjoyed throughout my career has been to work with teams from all over the world and I see from the vacancy notice that the position requires a manager with the ability to work in a culturally diverse environment.

During my time with the ... we were faced with the dilemma of encouraging staff to work together who had previously been on opposite sides of conflict. By introducing short morning meetings where everyone gave a one-minute report we created a working atmosphere where each member of the team could have their say without fear of judgement or criticism. In turn this resulted in strengthening the working relationships and helped us to achieve our objectives ahead of our deadline."

Always use examples that are relevant to the job to which you are applying and describe them in plain and simple language. And if you're concerned that you don't speak perfect English, please remember that English is *not* the native language for about 90 per cent of employees in the UN family.

Finish the letter with a couple of sentences along the lines of

"I look forward to meeting you and thank you for your kind consideration."

Remember not to 'brand' yourself according to a job title. Keep asking yourself these questions: what image to you want to promote? Which achievement(s) are you proud of? What do you do really well? Ask your family and friends about what *they* think your strengths are. Are you a good organizer? Are you good at details or are you more of a big picture person? Are you a team player or do you work better when you're on your own?

It might take a while to find all the answers and even longer to put them into simple sentences, but once you have created your profile/cover letter it will only need minor tweaks depending upon the job that you are applying for.

NOTES AND GREAT IDEAS

SIX - BRINGING IT ALL TOGETHER

"Do your little bit of good where you are; it's those little bits of good put together that overwhelm the world." – Desmond Tutu

You have almost finished …

After you have re-checked everything you have written so far you can begin to copy and paste your information into the online application form.

You may decide to use bullet points when setting out your work experience, and just make sure that your form is easy to read, splitting text into paragraphs if necessary. Our eyes need 'white space' to be able to interpret what we're reading.

Final suggestions:

1. Read the job application carefully. If the organisation is asking for a CV and not an online application form, send a CV. *Do not* use the application form of another employer.

2. Do not send a photograph unless specifically asked to do so. If you happen to be wearing a pink shirt in your photograph and the person looking at your application thinks that pink is a horrible colour, you could be putting yourself at a disadvantage.

3. Many online application platforms ask you whether you would like to be considered for other positions/locations. Be selective about which boxes you tick.

4. Keep a record of your applications, and always adapt/change an application to the specific requirements of a vacancy.

5. If you are submitting a form via email, ensure that you have the correct spelling of the person that you are sending your application to and remember to attach your form.

SEVEN - RESULT!

"You have brains in your head, you have feet in your shoes, you can steer yourself in any direction you choose." - Dr Seuss

Congratulations! You now have the basis of a fantastic CV or application, a document that will help employers understand how great you really are, and which will stand out, increasing your chances of an interview.

Of course some changes will still have to be made depending upon the job that you are applying for – remember to pick out and *include key words* relevant to the vacancy - but the majority of the hard work is behind you.

A final note on social media

There are no secrets on the internet, so check your social media platforms and pretend that you are a stranger looking at what is there. What impression do you get? Do some of those photographs or jokes need to be removed? Have your views on some subjects changed so that your Facebook posts no longer reflect the real you? Would you be prepared to see your posts on the front page of the newspaper?

'Google' yourself and go through the results because if they are interested, a potential employer will do it as well. If you find something that you rather were not there you can ask 'Google' to remove it.

Change your profile picture and use your social network to promote the image that you would like employers to see.

We're finished

If you have found this book useful please remember to write a review on Amazon. And if you'd like to stay in touch please come and connect with me on LinkedIn or on Facebook.

With all my heart I wish you every success in finding the job of your dreams in the UN family!

QUESTIONS AND ANSWERS

In this final section I have put together the questions that I get asked most frequently, together with my answers.

Question: I have gaps in my application because I was unemployed. What should I do?
Answer: This is one of those million dollar questions. If you were unemployed because of redundancy as a result of restructuring, merger etc., you can include this information. But then you must also describe what you have been doing during the time in question.

For example, reading the newspaper and meeting friends for coffee is not a great thing to write about. You might say instead that you have been using the time to continue your professional development, researching the job market, and networking. Did you do any volunteering or community work?

Question: I was ill for a long time so wasn't working. Should I include that on my CV?
Answer: Another tough one, because if you include information about being ill you could potentially put the employer off taking a closer look. This has to be a personal decision, but *don't go into details* about your state of health.

Question: Should I include the reason for wanting to leave my job?
Answer: Some organisations require an answer to this question. If you are leaving a job because you want to, you will hopefully have a good reason; 'I hated my boss', or 'I want a salary increase' are not things that an employer wants to read. Put yourself in the shoes of the person responsible for hiring; what would you accept as a valid reason for wanting to move on?

Question: Should I tell the truth?
Answer: ALWAYS!

Question: What should I talk about if I don't have any work experience because I'm only just leaving school/college/university?
Answer Focus on how quick you are to learn, and your strengths. Give examples of how you can take the initiative to get things done. Your answers are still going to have to show the employer how they will benefit from having you on board, and you need to paint a picture for them the same as anyone else.

ADDITIONAL READING AND USEFUL LINKS

Covey, S. (2004) "The 7 Habits of Highly Effective People: Powerful Lessons in Personal Change"

Hendricks, G. PhD (2009) "The Big Leap: Conquer Your Hidden Fear and Take Life to the Next Level"

Letherbarrow, G (2017) "Interviews and Videos: Present Like a Pro and Nail That Job!'

https://careers.un.org/lbw/Home.aspx

https://unjobs.org/

https://www.impactpool.org/search

www.businessballs.com

www.careerbuilder.com

www.cv.co.uk

www.glassdoor.com

www.idealist.com (great for internships and volunteer positions)

www.indeed.com

www.linkedin.com

www.linkup.com

www.mindtools.com

www.monster.co.uk or www.monster.com

Remember that in addition to looking at the website of individual companies it can be very useful to put your job title and location in to your internet search engine and go through the first couple of pages of results.

ABOUT THE AUTHOR

Gwyneth is the Creator of 'Stepping into You'™, Personal Branding Strategist, Author, Speaker, and Professional Development Coach. Her company, Feelgood Coaching and Consulting, focuses on using emotional intelligence to create brilliance.

In addition to her formal university studies she is a qualified coach and provides specialist coaching and consultancy services to help people define their own brand so that they market themselves successfully.

Gwyneth loves working with people – as opposed to machines - recognizing that each one of us is unique and is capable of creating a fabulous future according to our own values and desires.

The training and professional development of others has always been an integral part of Gwyneth's working life. She has over 25 years' experience within multi-national and multi-cultural environments such as the UN and the OSCE throughout Europe and the Balkans, as well as having worked in the private sector.

Other books by the same author:

Interviews and Videos: Present Like a Pro and Nail That Job!
Working Under Pressure: Emotional Intelligence in the Workplace

www.ingramcontent.com/pod-product-compliance
Lightning Source LLC
Chambersburg PA
CBHW081019240526
45471CB00017B/3422